Only Yesterday

Poems of Love Loss, and Life.

Lee F Robinson

The Manifesto Press Ltd

Directors: Lee F Robinson and June E Robinson

authorHOUSE®

AuthorHouse™
1663 Liberty Drive
Bloomington, IN 47403
www.authorhouse.com
Phone: 1-800-839-8640

First published by AuthorHouse   06/06/2011

ISBN: 978-1-4567-8194-1 (sc)
ISBN: 978-1-4567-8195-8 (ebk)

Printed in the United States of America

Any people depicted in stock imagery provided by Thinkstock are models, and such images are being used for illustrative purposes only.
Certain stock imagery © Thinkstock.

This book is printed on acid-free paper.

To Lee

Your words are scattered
Like stars against the night
From your long years
Brightness in your fading light

Familiar now your even script
On the envelope quickly ripped
Memory of the life you've lived
Treasured as a precious gift

In riotous India tongas rush
60 years as yesterday
Sailors brawl and lovers sing
In debauched, deadly Tiger Bay

Love and loss and love again
Old soldier by a lonely grave
Sam Helen's legion's marching by
Words of beauty never die

Alison Smith
09.10.10

Dedicated to my wife, June.

With thanks for great help from

Alison Smith

And

Clare Jackson and her team at Sunrise
Carol Elligott and her team at Sunrise

Only Yesterday
Poems of love, loss and life

Lee F Robinson

Lee F Robinson C.Eng MICE MAE MCIArb

Lee F Robinson was born in South Wales in 1923 and went to high school and college in Cardiff. During the Second World War he served as a Sapper at home and abroad.

He worked as an Engineer in Ferrous and non—ferrous metallurgy, and in the process industry in refineries and chemical plants. And even Biotechnology. A true Jack of All Trades! In latter years he was a consultant, mainly abroad for major firms and governments.

Lee has been happily married to June. for 36 years. They have three children each from previous marriages and live in a "Sunshine" Residence in Chorleywood—Herts.

Lee's poems chart a rich life from his humble beginnings in a South Wales mining village to India, Africa, Australia and many other places.
This is his first book.

Autumn 1939 was an important date for me. I started to read Engineering. I was introduced to Calculus, We had a beautiful Autumn with the leaves falling everywhere. I decided to write my first poem. And then also the Second Great War started.

Calculus in Autumn
Teacher and text book bred my conviction,
Of change, continuity, smoothest inflexion.
Observational points, in graph book and mind.
I joined them together with the smoothest of line.
Under the oak tree, straining to hear,
The source of a thousand pistol shots clear.
Each tiny crack was the death of a leaf.
Fracturing life—stem, infinitesimal, brief.
One moment attached, the next disconnected.
Discontinuity proven, the theory rejected.
Crystallized time in quick brittle break,
Not long the supple bend but the flint and the flake.

Home

The wind sang me to sleep, whilst yet a child.
Soft whistling around the bedroom walls of my recess
Whilst the aerial cable tapped gently upon my window.

We had **no** heat above the ground floor coal fires
Yet in **my** blankets close wrapped I lay happily
In **my** home, in the winds path between the sea
And the guardian hills I drifted content.

These fond memories ensured survival
Across the world in the burning heat and bitter cold,
War and turmoil, danger, injury and betrayal,
All soothed by the sweet recall of home.

Eighty years have passed since then
Sixty years since last I saw you.
Yet I sense its welcome, for the time,
Not long now approaches of my final return to my first and
ever Home.

2010

My Birthplace

As **my** valley moved to its uplands ending
So closed in the hills and steepened the sides
Whilst at its base a sluggish river gurgled
Impenetrable black, thickened with coal dust.

There on the narrowing strip a single road followed it
A few local shops, council yards, barbers
Where the land was wider a small, obsolete tin plate works
The "doublers" turning with tongs the red hot sheets
Striped to the waist, pouring sweat, drinking copious beer

Poised above, the great colliery wheels free dropped
Fresh colliers to the seams and drew **up** the grimy
Weary men at their days end. Full trams to the hoists and
Empty on their return to be filled again, drawn by pit ponies.

Twice the great horn blasts called the women to the shafts
Fear on their faces as they awaited the cages carrying
Stretchers of dead and wounded and their rescuers
From collapsed roofs—once from a methane explosion.

Above, atop the hills, ever increasing and spreading
The cones of the colliery washings, fine coal, rock and slate
Menacing as it increased the threat to bury
All life that lay below, the cottages in strips bitten
Into the sides, like rows of false teeth.

No pit baths in those days, houses welcomed the men
With tin baths fed with steaming hot water by wives
To their husbands and sons to blackening bath towels
Ready laden tables—then to the pubs.

Yes, I did return, long after, to see my play ground
Row upon row of empty streets, cottages boarded up
The colliery structures gone or going, the tin sheet works demolished
Gone were the shops, only one shabby pub left.

No male voice choir sung 'Cwm Rhondda, no roaring colliery brass band
Broke the unnatural silence. Only aged colliers Sitting on benches
Spitting black phlegm from their ruined lungs, as they gossiped
Of the young men who had departed the flatlands and the coast
"Du it was hard, hard. Harder than they will ever know."
Heroes all.

2 October 1010

My Boots

At the end of summer holidays I had outgrown my boots,
My father took them to the local cobbler to sole and heel,
My mother carefully polished and wrapped them for me,
As other fortunate to take to first day of elementary term.

An unforgettable scene: as the hall was filled with piles of boots,
Of ragged children in their fathers cut down trousers,
Sitting in rows of benches. Our 'old maid' teachers on their knees,
Pulling and pushing to fit where they could on black, bare feet.

For the winter would come as the unemployed's children walked
Through snow and ice with bruised and bloodied feet to school
Some post war children know hardship but these knew distress
Often boots within a day were pawned for a fag and a drink

But our police provided a hand punch and brass eyelet
Machine and the brokers knew once caught their license was gone.
How many you ask were thus deprived? At least half, who came
To school on a glass of water but were saved by the free pinta.

Good old days? Like hell they were! And what was the turning point?
Rearmament that called for men to work and earn,
Who had been unwanted scrap.
For children to eat, wash dress in proper clothes,
Grow strong enough to serve and saved this nation.

12 December 2010

Where It began

I was an outsider looking with envy on the group of confident
Class mates who walked around the Parks outer path as dusk fell.
Crossing and re-crossing the groups of girls, chafing and joking
Displaying, whilst the boys leader asked his contacts of the willingness,
Or otherwise of any new face amongst the girls. Whilst we listened,
With admiration at his confident boldness.

I had always been an outsider when suddenly one evening
I became a member of the Pack. Somehow we joined up with girls
One by one and equally in pairs peeled of till I found myself
Alone with a quiet girl, that to me was beautiful beyond compare.
I was struck silent but I plucked up courage to take her hand
Which she did not withdraw but let it lay quietly within mine.

We found our selves, not consciously, in one of the many unlit lanes,
That backed the house garden walls whilst here and there we heard
The murmured sounds of love, of laughter and occasional protest.
Till we found an area of quiet, aloneness and secret desire.
She lay back back against a door, I pressed my lips on hers,

Which remained shut, but neither did she turn away from
mine.

I felt her body through her clothes my head pulsing,
throbbing,
And not discouraged, sought to insert my hands within her
clothes,
Until all that I had seen in books, paintings, was revealed as
true
More wonderful than my wildest imagination. She lay quiet
neither
Encouraging or rejecting my clumsy naivety. Then quietly
spoke,
"I suppose you think you are very clever." That brought me to
my senses,
We parted with my making urgent dates to meet again,
agreed.

She never came. Nor did I ever see her again with the girl
packs.
But my first experience remained a fantasy of delight,
For which I remain ever grateful to her.

22 Nov.2010

Yes Headmaster

He was an imposing figure, tall, slim, elegant
With his black gown and red hood.,
When he strode from his office into the hall
To glare down on the three of us idly chatting.

Unprepared, when he pointed an accusing finger
And demanded "Which one of you stole the little men?"
"Bird, I know it was a shock headed Peter like,
You." Faced with madness we sought each others eyes.

He was eccentric,—but little men, gnomes, pixies?
Obviously off his rocker.— It suddenly occurred to me.
We were organized in games houses each with a colour
To our Name. Up four ladders climbed little men
Each bearing our rugby jerseys, awarded weekly points.

"If it's the point earners have gone, Sir, We are Hawke
And in the lead;-So its more likely to be loosers
Like Drake or Raleigh rather than a Hawke man."
"Robinson, I do not like your amoral reasoning!

Some of his subject at daily assembly were strange,
"I came in this morning my heart lifted high
By The beautiful spring weather, and what do I see,?
But a filthy phlegm in the middle of the yard.
Savages is what I teach savages!"

Some months later in another group listening to the great
Clifford Iltydd as he played a girls school Group like fish upon a
line, Something in a tall girls face took his attention.
"What's your name darling? ""Clarissa" Yes, but your surname?
"I knew it, I knew the face" and throwing honeyed words over his
Shoulder, we gained ladder points for rapid disengagement.!
Little Man! Oh Little Men.

MyDoc; Yes Headmaster Lee.F.Robinson 28 Dec 2010

Fair Interval

To my friend Stuart who died too young.

My friend had no need
To part his lips in smile,
For the sparkle of his eyes
Sufficient made the jest.

Because all his blood line
Waited to greet him at the passing.
It is both fit and right
That I, at least, should mourn him.

Who has no wife or child,
To tell of what he was
Before the days of fading,
And what he might have been.

When all the future easy lay
Like time, within his palm,
To grasp upon the moments will,
Before it vanished in the grip.

I watched him confidently stride,
Towards his rightful recognition,
Of fame and honour rising
Like the certain summer sun.

No later act I wish recall,
This part I choose him speak,
Then yesterday was but the shortest way
And endless, were the easy paths of morrow.

Memory

He lies outside there now, sleeping peacefully.
In dreams it is ever spring; for the earth
Is a warm cloak. Yet we, unmercifully,
Grow old, and fear the winter's birth.

Now that the summers gone; fled is our joy.
The wind, howling at us from every barren tree,
Sings only softly, a sweet, vague familiar melody,
To his receptive ears.

The rose petals that caress the ground,
Garland him gently, honour bound,
To tell the sweet seasons passing.

The sun seeking birds in their flight,
Each year have I seen rest at this same spot.
True to their custom. The fading light
Paying their tribute. The yearly lot
of News. So that he will not lonely lie,
When we too are gone.

1947

Street Scene

With the dusk streets spring to life as the heat dissolves
Into the bustling, jostling, competing for a way between
The tongas, the bikes, the sacred cows—
Munching their gifts of cabbage leaves whilst more
And more garlands are hung about their willing necks.

The air so heavy with a hundred spices from open sacks
Upon earth floors, where sat cross-legged the village
storekeepers
Offering their samples of simple sweets of boiled sugar cane
With beaming smiles and pleasure and many blessings
The ringing of the temple bells clashing with the frantic
bikes.

Everywhere people. Half naked children scrambling in the
mud,
The young girls displaying their cheap but so colourful saris
Swinging their hips before the young men
Watched by careful mothers, whilst their husbands draw on
biris
Held upright between fingers. Or chewing betel
To give mouths dyed red round bright white teeth.

22 July 2010
Sixty years as nothing! Memory hold the door!

Tongas—horse drawn two wheeled taxi
Biris—self rolled cigarettes from tobacco leaves

The Chariotee'r

The prince tested his bow, well beyond a normal mans strength
As he gazed along the endless ranks of eager warriors
Foot soldiers, archers, horseman above all charioteers
To replace his own dead driver.

Distracted by the strange, soft sound of a flute
From between the ranks by a slender herdsman
Approaching with many a bow and whispered
"Great Lord, I would be your charioteer."

Laughing the Prince replied "You control these great steeds?"
Turned to study the ranks, when yet again the flute sang out
And the great white steeds moved to the player
Pawing the ground, nuzzling him, softly neighing
Overriding the tug of the Prince's pull upon the reins.

For the briefest of moments a shaft of light tinged with blue
The youths light fawn, his eyes flashed red, teeth shining
As never seen before. The Prince was forced to ask
"Could you control these massive horses against their will?"
"Never my Lord. Yet I can play and sing them to your
desire."

The Prince stood aside casting the reins to the youth
Who vaulted swiftly into the chariot, and thousands followed
As he drove towards their kinsman—enemies, whilst the
Prince
Was full of doubts as to whether even his grievance
Could possibly justify the destruction of all this host.

11 October 2010

The Eagle's Eye

From the gap in the cloud at great height
The human vision would see only an anthill
And the sprinkling of black dots
Against the sand.

From his great eyes, across his wing tips
The Eagle saw the gathering of armies
Kinsman and enemies
At one and the same time.

Soldiers, foot and horse,
Chariots and great steeds
Waiting a call of the Archer Prince
Midway between his kinsman
To commence battle

He lifted his eyes to the hills and cried
"I am become Death
The Destroyer of Worlds"
And gave the order to advance.

4 October 2010

My Tiger and My Party

Tiger bay, **in** its day, had a reputation, particularly amongst the merchant seamen worldwide, as a tough and dangerous area, with a large red light district.

It started with the development of Cardiff docks as the largest coal exporting port in the world. By 1913, it was exporting no less than 9 million tons a year of Welsh steam coal, mainly in locally owned steam tramp ships.

In the 1800s seamen began to marry and have a house where his family lived whilst he made his voyages. The area was said at the turn of the century to have 45 different nationalities, including Somali, Spanish, Italian, Yemeni, Caribbean, Norwegian etc.

As the coal industry declined after 1950 the docks closed and were converted to marinas. The houses of Tiger Bay were demolished and the occupants dispersed to new housing estates to be replaced by the National Assembly, concert halls and up market hotels. And fewer and fewer people survive who actually walked there and can remember The Bay.

August 2010

My Tiger and My Party

Oh what would by mother have said
Had she known where her 16 year old
Dodged his supposed night at the pictures
And changing trams to reach the den of iniquity
Tiger Bay!

Oh the thrill! To sit in the bar of seamen and whores
Singing and stamping to the old piano
Demanding of "Abie, Abie my boy
What are you waiting for now?"
"More promising to be with you
In apple blossom time, my dear
To change your name to mine."

Saving my pocket money for the day of
Forbidden pleasure. A long time coming!
My worldly wise elder brother said
"Why buy a cow when milk is free?
Besides less chance of a dose!"

How right he proved. With enthusiastic amateurs
The thrilling, the willing, experienced *****~girls
Ready to teach novices.
When once I joined the party.
My first night in bed . . . unforgettable
Unique. Unexpected. Wonderful.
Like never forgetting how to ride a bike.

I learnt fast. Like how the greatest insult was
One of our black comrades calling another
"You're just a white man!"

Our collar and tie black group leader
"Why everyone knows me."
The kids in the street call out
"Hullo Harry, How de do?"

Lascars walked half naked down the street
A girl on each arm.
Screaming and noise of fighting and love
Poured from every open window.
This racial mixture, the excitement, this heaven!

We had our remnants of lumpen proletariat
'This party is getting too bourgeois
Like that fellow***
He's bourgeois he is
What I says is, chuck him out!"

Our district organiser, round and soft of features and of
voice,
Of winning smile, had often to move
"A most hearty Vote of Censure" on one or another
Of his argumentative defiant flock
"Left-wing infantilism" he called it.

Our young but massive new copper
On his first patrol, attacked by six yobbos,
Laid them all out along the kerb
Like a set of well bowled ninepins.

Oh my Tiger and my Party intertwined
What fun and so soon to go
Forever, never to return

You planners, you ripped it all down
Dispersed its people
For expensive restaurants and 'cultural buildings'
Hives for bureaucrats, politicians and other scum

In memory they remain
The Tiger and The Party
The Party and The Tiger
What fun we had. What fun!
Au revoir!

4 August 2010

Stockholm

In the early 70s I was employed as a consultant to the Ministry of Industry of the Swedish Govt on a number of occasions. I frequently stopped at Stockholm.

Although a modern city there was one of the islands which was entirely covered with medieval buildings, mostly empty, above ground but led to a whole series of interconnected cellars used as restaurants—long wooden tables where you sat in rows together. When one left it was to a maze of ill lit narrow streets, dark arches, winding this way and that. Once such moonlit night, the streets white with snow in the early hours of the morning, I had strange visions of beings in the doorways and arches. The poem is not realistic, not narrative but a description of the emotions I experienced.

I did not imagine the 'beings' in the arches. I was well aware they were tricks of the moonlight and a few flickering gas lights.

Stockholm

Cloaked and faceless is the man
Who hugs a pivoting skeleton
Its image etched by the moon
Upon the rough stone
Silver tinting the cobbles

Enveloping satin
Swathes the body and boney whilst
The skull wears a twisted grin
Black white its clowns daub
But the faceless one? Nothing.

Yet and yet the very blankness
Hides a deep menace
The exposed bones
Have no grimace but
A strange silence prevails.

The moon paints shadows
As breezes rustle the cloak
Whilst feet caress the ground
The old bones swing slack
And a distant thunder shakes the clouds.

You ill assorted pair!
Hidden in the deep recesses
Motionless, both exposed and hidden
Long gone are your features
Why do you beckon me?

October 1973

Sarn Helen

I felt a drive to say something in poetry that had significance,
More than merely pretty pictures, even if it was highly likely
I would fail. The subject sprang from reading a little of the
Roman Roads constructed by the legions in Wales The main
road; Isca Silurum from East to West which connected with
the South to North Coastal Road; Sarn. Helen.

Beneath the heather it was often a mere indistinct track with
slabs appearing here and there beneath the heather. And
containing some steep climbs.

There appeared little or none in the way of buildings of that
era and the purpose was not occupation but movement of
minerals , in particular Gold.

Welsh Gold was much sort after and still is mined in small
quantities to this very time.

There is a little I could read about the nomadic cattle owning tribes and even less about any relationship with the Romans and their legions. The Romans were not interested in subduing very scattered people with land they did not wish to occupy. The Celtic tribes had no interest in attacking a force far beyond their capability. There was nothing in the way of a struggle as with the Druids of North Wales and their well organised society'

If their was a Celtic–Romano civilisation (which Mortimer Wheeler doubted, it had precious few relics in this part of central mountainous Wales with hardly any villages or garrison towns like Caerleon.

My uninformed guess is they largely ignored one another. This was a poor attempt to see how each saw the other, which interested me

If a failure at least I tried, and enjoyed doing it!

Sarn Helen

We of the Mother City—also mercenaries
Of vine and corn and friendly sun
Marched from river, meadow and woods
Across blind shrouded uplands
Barren soil, needle grass, heather bog
Till suddenly—through twisted rocks
Black, tortured, stumps and gorse
We saw dark waves and steep descent
Sank our way in soft white sand.

We marched—so that a message went
Horse sweat by horse sweat to Imperial Throne
That we, a lost legion, could no further go,
We stood upon the ultimate an unknown
The report was but half-heard, misunderstood
Dismissed with boredom and a yawn, swiftly
Extinguishing the record of our suffering
Our loneliness and longing for our homes.
No record was inscribed in honour of our going.

No reason was ever given for our journey,
We marched westward as the arrow flight.
Because the land sloped ever upwards
Into an unmapped trackless waste.
To seek a limit to the landmass
Circumscribe the boundaries of quaint time
There we waited the foam of a keel heave
From hilltops eagerly sought the hearth smoke
And all was still and sightless to our grief.

So as the leaf fall foretold the winter

We closed our ranks and stepped out
The path we came, erecting and claiming
By cairns our marked way, random
But straight. As befits our veterans
Through mud and water, mire and bracken
The early unwelcome winter of Black Mountains
Cut rivulets of ice rain in furrowed cheekbone
Twisted with jest the fingers of our night frost.

The silence was broken rare by vixen scream
Moor bird, owl screech and the crunch
Of heather at nightfall. By unknown stirrings
Beneath our very bodies as we tired lay
Yet through the swirling misty peaks
Our sharp eyed ones saw, on distant beacons
Solitary, indistinct crouched figures, watching
Or so they said. Earth merged immovable
Yet on a second view there were no more.

All of us, along our march route
Saw the hoof tracks of ponies in mud freeze
The droppings of large sheep herds
But the riders and the shepherds saw we none

Suddenly, a standing stone raised by alien hand
Erected, carved with wreathed and twisted knots
Patterns so complex, intersected, ancient, mysterious
That made the mind reel. The green mossed granite
Of a strange hue. Although alone, we were not yet alone.

The descent was pleasant. Step by step
Shorter and softer the footfall to our heart

The lapping rivers edge, the palisaded camp
The limb reviving bath, the wine and oil
Bread, altar and the upward lifting laugh
Of womenfolk, forgot and children's play
The smell of leather polished. Burnishing
Of brass. This duty and familiar routine
Filled now our days. The dreamland was forgot.

The Second Legion
We the practical men, engineers sound in mind
Strong in limb saw the first legion shipped to Gaul
Veterans to the plough, young men to fighting frontiers
Ambitious Praetorians to Rome. Sickness lay
Heavy on their sleep. Haunted by lack of seeing
Emptiness and Void. Or so they claimed.
But we laid well the chariot slab, fastened the mire
We cleft the moorland with hammering
From cairn to cairn we threaded through the way.

Before the road had reached its salty end
The orders came to turn from West to North
To deal with insurrection and revolt
Speedily put down in North and South
Amongst the valleys and mountain peaks
For on our road the chariots, horse and foot
Proceeded to the wars. But as they traversed on
The moorlands, uplands and the middle land
We met no opposition saw no sign of life.

Along the road we build few forilets, no villas
Staging posts, nor lodge. But lead and gold
Above all gold, we mined and so we kept

The road repaired until the drift of men
Began towards the vortex of the world
The sickening spin and emptying down
The plug of civilisation withdrawn. Whirlpool
Of endless chaos, wild barbarians, bloodshed
Wreck and wrack, discord and the dark.

The Watchers

We watched their arrival with wry amusement
And their going without sincere regret
This is not their land nor is it ours
But we are of it. We make no settlements
No walls to crumble, roof beams to fall
Wandering freely over the wild waste land
Knowing each tortuous step by day and night
Reading the messages of our kinsfolk
Where and when our future meeting place.

We had no home. We had a thousand homes
Our caves and hollows. Windbreak of taught hide
Floors of deep furs, secure against the cold
We slept the long nights and at first light
Took our women, face down, in the deep warmth
Slept again until he sun's rise awoke
Our hearts. Wa.watched the strangers grovel at Daulocothi
For gold dust by mule loads—whilst we
Handed down circlets, elder to elder, age to age.

We were before them, man and ghost, before the swordsmen
Before the hauliers of rocks. We were the first men.
As we shall be the last. The road sunk deep
Beneath the bracken. No one treads but soft feet

As we meander through the uplands
Cross and recross the hearts yearn
Few in numbers, rarely meeting, ever present
In the mistland, people in the past time
Enshrined in mystic legend and the Bardic song.

November 1973

Sea Winds Song

The cowardly sailors decry my howl and roar
As wave top to wave top I dance towards the shore
Gathering salt spray, till I crash upon the beach
Flinging the sand to ridge and furrow my reach.

One final leap, to mount the cliff and bend the gorse
As in the field I trample the grass down to the earth
Ignoring hedges to burst into the gardens and the paths
Leaving my fingerprint in salt upon the glass.

Tomorrow the housewife will try to wipe away
But only smear the salty marks and wonder
Whence it came, whilst I rush on to the waiting hills
Climbing and widening and softening as I go.

For I am the gale and brother to the rain
Sister to the clouds, asleep till I come again.

20 June 2010

The Heartland

White on black and black on white
Barred sky, gaunt poplars stand
Rank upon rank, silent band
Awaits the clarion call of spring
To life and leaf and bud.

When that awakening comes
Shall we once more respond?
Or shall the sap of life
Frozen and still remain.

This land is harsh, the soil is thin
The trees are mean and barely cling
With tenuous roots on fractured stone,
Between the boulders wildly thrown.

But still, this is our heartland
Where we walked of old
Upon the ridges and the knife edge
Rocks, whence bled our feet and froze
Our flesh in winter, and in summer
Burnt, cracked and parched our flesh
Whilst crevices threatened sting and fang
Against the cautious step.

The dark and sullen caves disputed
For shelter, home or even resting place
With bear, the tiger and the boar
Sealing possession with spouse fire.

From baffled brow the deep set eyes
Looked down and down
To where the soil was rich
The woods were ripe
Seas lapped the shore
Of mellow seasoned sand
Soft to the touch and foot
And honey, berries, corn and wine
Lay to the hand to easy take.
Fallen leaves and carpet mass
In shaded sun and gentle ways
Deep in desire and untold ease.

Why then remain in these harsh heights
Unyielding and disjoint of season
To strive to kill and die, dispute
With each and all such meagre fruit.
Was this an act of folly or of spleen?
Did then it spring from some perverted pride?
Or did you seek with instinct or of guile
To breed a people harshly wrought
In iron will and body, to survive
The tempests, fire and chill of this wild world?
To suffer, starve yet finally survive
Subdue, dominate, divide what waits below.

This was our heartland, where we grew
From child to man, and now
From man to child, we there renew.

June 1978

Catraeth

Following **the** withdrawal of the Romans, Britain became the battleground between the dominant Celtic Kingdoms and the invading Anglo Saxons. Northumbria was then a Celtic Kingdom linked to the Celtic Kingdoms of what is now Wales. The Anglo Saxons made inroads north of the Humber and the last ditch attempt to stop the invaders was made by Mynyddog, King of the Gododdoin, who drew on Celtic warriors from a wide area, to attack the main Anglo Saxon base at Catraeth, near modern day Catterick.

This was a total disaster and it was said that of the force of 300 princely horsemen and retainers only three survived! This spelt the end of the Celtic Kingdoms of the north which became universally Anglo Saxon. The dates is uncertain and disputed but is somewhere around 590ad.

Catraeth

The Song of King Mynyddog

Half blind, old.
Who now will sing my praise?
A feared warrior
Great King.

Does not my name mean luxury?
Who is more famed for wealth?

Weep for the King Mynyddog,
Grieve for his old age.

From my stronghold of Din Eydin,
High rock seat of Arthur
Looked I upon my fair lands.
From a palace cloaked in riches,
Gold, silver and royal purple
Were the halls—all perfume filled
With fairest of smooth women.

The Kingdom was extended
To the limits of ambition.

When Mynyddog towered skyward
Above his watchful warriors,
Keeping boundaries inviolate,
Till blindness overtook me.
The warriors grew they fewer

With corruption of our seed.

Gone are fair illusions,
Fled are hopes of future,
Of inheritance of princes,
Palaces that stand.
Longing only for survival
Till a quiet decent grave.

To my great feast they have hastened
The flower of Goddodin,
Fairest of all princes
Stripling Lords of Brython,
Favourite sons of Gwen!.

My warriors were like fine gold
Embraced by loathsome clay,
Swallowed in filthy mud,
Of the heathen, of the Anglo Saxons

Oozing in their sullen way
Squat, ungainly, leather covered
Breeding, ever breeding,
In coarseness of their blood.

Come hasten to Din Eydin.
To Mynyddog's great feast.
To gifts beyond all measure.
To the mead horn,
To your death.

The song of the Warriors

We rode together, who would ride with no other.
Three hundred princes of Celtic host
Golden, the shimmering circlets of our necks.
Green our cloaks streaming in the wind.

Laughing accompanies our horses stride.
Echo the moorland of Northumbria.
Listen hills and valleys to our song.
You shall not hear their like again.

We come with honour and with mead
Upon our lips. Within our breath
The kiss of dark red wine
Caresses of the fairest women of Din Eydin.

Twelve months have we feasted,
In the hall of King Mynyddog.
Luxurious, open handed
Now we shall repay him.

Twelve months the drinking horns
Passed brimming yellow mead,
Amongst the warriors of Brython.
The women moaned by firelight.

Mynyddog asked nothing of us.
We go because a year has gone,
Because of bondage in our honour
Because we read his secret thoughts.

We have risen and donned coats,
Shining, of dull grey mail.
Girded swords of blue, with hilts of deeper blue.
Shields, bull hide, lime whitened to the boss.

Catraeth, to you we ride.

The Sentry

You have mocked the sentry on the wall,
Your civilisation will fall, fall, fall!

He walked the ramparts chilled and underfed
Far from you thoughts in warm and silken bed
Except as a butt for cowardly, sneering, jest
Of his slow wit—for you know best
How to avoid his harsh and patient toil
In guarding the freedom of your fathers' soil.

You have called him dolt and called him swine,
Your vaunted superiority will soon decline.
Beyond the wall and within the gate
Barbarians stir with greed and hate.
They long to burn, they lust for rape
Their swords will clip your curly nape.
What keeps the wolf from the sheep like flock?
Only the sentry that you mock!

You call him drunkard, lout and thief.
The sentry quietly takes his leave.

Over the wall, without, within
The faceless horde are swarming in
The crops alight, the doors are down
How you scream for the drunken clown!

Return! Return! And save our skin
From the slashing knife of our savage kin

The Sentry has left the lonely wall
Your civilisation will fall, fall, fall!

May 1978

Love Poem

Suddenly, she sat bolt upright, out of our warmth.
Into the full spring moonlight; whilst I lay curious
But content, studying the dappled curves
Kissed by each cloud. In silence, waited.

Then a ringing of her hands, not in joy nor in sorrow
And then? Removing a ring from her fingers.
The arching of back and arm and sudden release
And springing breast. Out flew the ring,
Down the moonbeam, through the window.

Whilst into the smoothness—the body perfume
Into my memory, forever, please remain
My moonlight. Who kissed the grace of my lover's body.

The ring made no noise on its arrival,
In hell for all I care or still circling forever,
The pathway of betrayal, of love unearned

Making room for an ever deeper passion
Which time I knew must mellow
Into that valley of content
Of bodies painted, arranged, sculpted
By our spring moonlight memory.

Now stolen by the villain—age!

Let it return one last time?
A useless longing when
Only moonlight remains.

June 1972

Lone Lake

Softly, silently, leaving my partner sound asleep,
I padded my way, To the balcony,
Unconsciously, Called by the singing wind?
Watching the moonlight dance from ripple to ripple
Shore to raft, Where mounted a blur of whiteness,
As the Swan climbed to Safety From Predatory Fox
Or Wandering Dog, adrift from home.

A distant call of hunting owl, answered by others.
So often heard, So rarely seen.
Drifting black clouds dapple the painted moon
Wrapped in happiness at my place and time. Desiring
No other. Never dreaming the end of my content
Leaving unsought, For Unknown slow descent;
From all my life that mattered.
Goodnight.

L.F. Robinson
December 2010·

COMPLINE.

Is this the cleft valley
That you fear to enter?
Where Dew—laden Gras
Shows no Footstep.?

Where Bird Songs, Hang:
Trapped in Breathless Air.

The great Hawks Wings
In the dark trees,
Are Motionless spread.

The stream Absorbs
In Depthless Black,
Un-reflected light.

Yes, I will enter,
Walk the lone paths,where
No meetings forebode

Save my own—self,
Shrouded in mist—wreath,
Trapped in Silence,
Emerging, Unrecognised

L.F. Robinson
Sept. 1975

I decided I could make much more sense by using the word "SUNRISE" in both senses at once, as the physical rising of the sun and the Senior Citizens Organisation.
I have also turned it in the way of optimism for the old as for the young.

HAIKU-SUNRISE

SUNRISE at young life
Awakens a great joyfulness
In old age also

SUNRISE, birth of spring
Years death in Winter Darkness.
Green buds, from white ice.

SUNRISE returning
Takes us all by sharp Surprise.
All ends if absent.

Golden Age

Teetering and tottering
Stretching for the doorpost
Remembering the last fall
And the fractured bones.

"Can I help you mount the kerbstone?
"How kind of you, how kind."
But do I look so helpless
So idiotic too?

Deeply thankful but bitter to the taste.

The first time, the worst time, frozen
Standing on the pavement, something felt quite wrong
Digging in my feet, grasping at the thin air
Knowing it was coming

Then crashing to the floor.

Progressing from one stick to a second
A three wheel trolley next became my way
Wondering when a wheelchair
Would become my lot.

Am I the man who sprinted the assault course?
Vaulting over fence rails
To the instructors cry.
If I new the ending

Would I have begun?

Yes my brain is active
Is that an advantage?
Better to know inevitable descent
Than remain in happy ignorance?

24 June 2010

Saw frost laden Spiders Webb this morning. Then the Sun play upon it. Could not resist it.

THE MASTER BUILDER AND THE MASTER JEWELLER

Exhausted by his great effort the Master Builder rested in cool
And Darkness of a curled leaf. His structure was as always to the same plan
Embossed unconsciously on his tiny brain, yet always adapted in size
And Angle by the branches, the leaves, the sprigs and spurs of his trap.

Resting fearlessly, as his silken cables attached to his legs to warn
If any part of his tensed net began to quiver by a struggling intruder.
The morning dew coated each thread with strings of tiny clear drops,
That once the sun rose became tiny prisms of rainbow jewels,
Rubies, Emeralds, Sapphires, Diamonds in long strings,
Colours that attracted and snared a large grey Moth.

The Master Builder swung on a new spun thread like a trapeze,
To near the straining point. Spinning thread upon thread around
The struggler until it was a helpless parcel, to be wrapped
And passed along the net to the leaf nest for timely consuming.
A silken thread hundreds of times as strong as mans best effort.

The Master Jeweler laid out his wares upon white linen, gleaming,
Below the flickering Chandeliers, strings of Rubies, Emeralds,
Sapphires and Diamonds, masterpieces of his art. Women of Leisure
Looked in longing at his wares, and one in particular spoke of her
Longing, but the outreach of his price. The Master Jeweler whispered
"Visit my rooms tonight and let us see if for you alone we discount the price."

On the next party she won the admiration of her friends
For her new display. "Your husband must admire you so!"
"Oh he never has regarded me as a victim,
Ensnared by my Beauty, or that in a night a woman is worn out."

LANDSCAPE?

Could so small, a hidden, grove bear weight of" Landscape"?
A slope between banks a stream drifting down, I could
Step across, but only ankle deep, in clearest, sweetest water
That I strained to hear, gently burbling around the pebbles.

At the bottom of the fall, three ponds, water kissing from one,
To another and suddenly as it had arisen disappeared
Into soft green mossy ground too delicate to bear a foot,
Without destroying its tiny flowers of white and pink.

The whole in the gently moving shadows of the shrubs that lined
The Bank tops, never allowing the harsh light of a rampant sun.
To disturb the everlasting peace of place and mind,
Within its tiny shell to welcome rest, for one alone.

Look carefully, to see Kingdoms, within the ponds of hardly
Visible shrimp like creatures. In season the jellied eggs become the
Black dot tadpoles wriggling their way from side to side.
The indifferent frog parents had gone to larger living space.

There,there! A flash of blue and gold and rainbow shimmer of a
Kingfisher, come to inspect the likelihood of fish, but all too small.
But following the line of his departure the finches, and many
Small birds lose their colors as they rise into the sunlight.

In the world stretching beyond vision, beyond comprehension

Is there a place for the small, the gentle, the easily forgotten"
To dwell within a little place and little drifting thought,
Where merged the past, the present and future dreams.

And could it be rewarded with the great title of Landscape?

Prologue or Epilogue?

The Pearl forms in the Shell,
The Thought forms in the Miind.
The grit folds in the Pearl,
The sorrow stills the Thought.

The thought enshrines the Pearl,
The mind wrapped in the Shell.
The begining in the end,
The grit became the sorrow.

STRANGER

Wild Stranger! Who are you?
The plaything of a capricious God.

From Whence?
Wherever the Wind has blown me.

To What purpose?
All that was gained. was lost.

What then your name?
Why! - Call me Job.

Nearly 90 years and what have I learnt.?

Best summed up by Ecclesiastes.

Ecclesiastes

The race is not to the Swift.
Nor the battle to the Strong.
Nor yet honour to the Wise.
Or riches to the Diligent.

But Time and Circumstance determine all.